The Impea[chment of]
Barack Obama
and Hillary Clinton

For High Crimes in
Syria and Libya

By Michael Ostrowski
and
James Ostrowski

Cazenovia Books

Buffalo (USA)

LibertyMovement.org

Published by Cazenovia Books, Buffalo, New York

Front cover photo reprinted with permission of Reuters.

Back cover photo courtesy of the State Department

Printed in the United States of America

ISBN-13:978-0-9749253-1-8

First Edition July 2016

Dedication

To our high school coach, Bob Ivory, who inspired a generation of young men to go beyond themselves with his simple exhortation, "It's yours if you want it!"

"State is the name of the coldest of all cold monsters. Coldly it lies; and this lie slips from its mouth: 'I, the state, am the people.'

"The state lies in all the tongues of good and evil; and whatever it says it lies; and whatever it has it has stolen."

— Friedrich Nietzsche

Contents

Foreword

I have been lucky in the family department. I have had a great family to be sure, but I have also had some unusual opportunities to work with family members. I tried two First Amendment cases with my late father, William J. Ostrowski, after he retired from thirty years on the bench. I coached my son Will in baseball and basketball for many years. Now, my brother Mike and I have co-written this important book.

Truth is indeed stranger than fiction. I should point out that many years ago, we co-authored a screenplay that predicted the end of the war on drugs. Since that prediction is on the slow road to being fulfilled, I take that as a good omen for the success of this book.

I wrote many articles on foreign policy around the time of 9/11 and afterwards. As the years dragged on and the endless wars continued, I got disgusted and drifted off into writing about domestic issues. In the last few years, Mike got me going again by keeping me apprised of Obama's and Hillary's latest shenanigans in the Middle East, particularly in Syria and Libya. His take was typical Mike, contrarian, bold, cutting edge, incisive. The idea for this book arose out of those many conversations. And the rest is history.

* * * * *

A special thanks to Scott Horton of Antiwar Radio for his many valuable suggestions.

Jim Ostrowski

July, 2016

i

Introduction

In mid-2016, Americans face the threat of terrorism at home, endless war abroad in the Middle East and a refugee crisis that threatens to overwhelm Europe *and* America. Two people bear the most responsibility for this state of affairs. One is the incumbent President; the other has about a 50 percent chance to become the next President.

This is a dreary and dangerous predicament we find ourselves in. What is to be done? To sit on the sidelines and allow the nation to be dragged down ever further into the abyss is unthinkable. The Framers of the Constitution provided a legal and political mechanism for just such extreme cases of official misconduct.

This book makes the case for the commencement of impeachment proceedings against President Barack Obama and the former Secretary of State Hillary Clinton *in the event that she is elected President.* As of the date of publication, her odds of being elected are better than fifty-fifty. If the publication of this volume lessens those odds, that is all to the good.

Impeachment proceedings are commenced when the House of Representatives agrees to open an investigation of whether grounds exist to file articles of impeachment. A special committee is then appointed to undertake the investigation. After the investigation is completed, the committee votes on whether to send articles of impeachment to the full House of Representatives. The House is the master of its own rules on impeachment including the standard of proof needed to bring charges.

Impeachment is often compared to an indictment wherein the standard of proof is probable cause, more probable than not. However, the House applied a higher standard, "clear and convincing evidence," in deciding whether to impeach Richard Nixon. An even lower standard is appropriate for merely opening an investigation. That is because, prior to a formal investigation, many of the critical facts are unknown and *may be carefully hidden by the miscreants*. This is necessarily a judgment call. In the present instance, sufficient facts have been ferreted out by journalists and researchers to lead reasonable people to suspect that two illegal wars have been initiated for improper purposes and based on false information. Only a formal investigation by a House committee can cut through the fog of war and clandestine operations and reveal the true facts of these events. Thus, this book is a sustained argument for opening such an investigation.

The authors are not naïve about the prospects for such an investigation being approved by the House. Our opinion of the House is as low as anyone's. Many in the House likely approved the suspects' projects in Libya and Syria and with the exception of the attack on the consulate in Benghazi, have expressed little or no interest in investigating them. As of today, there is zero political will to initiate impeachment proceedings. However, history shows that what is politically impossible one day can become politically mandatory the next.

There are some good men and women in the House of Representatives and it is to them and to the American people that this volume is initially addressed. A copy of this book will be forwarded to each Member of the House so they cannot deny being put on notice of these charges. At the end of the day, the authors are only responsible for what *they* do, not what others do.

A Note on "Archism"

In writing this book, we concluded it was necessary, in describing what happened and why in Libya and Syria, to introduce a word that, if not a neologism, is certainly an obscure term used in what we believe is a novel manner: *archism*.

The state is a monopoly on the use of force in a region that supports itself with taxation. The absence of a state is referred to as "anarchy." It is a widespread belief that states are needed for civilization to exist. We are also led to believe that in the absence of a state, endless violence and chaos will ensue. States have had a good press for a long time. That may be because in most countries, the state has controlled the press directly or indirectly.

On the other hand, the notion that anarchism—the absence of states—might be a good thing is a relatively recent development. The most popular and best known form of anarchist theory, anarcho-syndicalism, does not really posit anarchy at all since it smuggles the state back into the picture and merely renames it the "collective" or the "committee." The truer form of anarchy, individualist anarchy or anarcho-capitalism is far less well known. The first anarcho-capitalist work was published in 1849.[1] In modern times, anarcho-capitalism has never been considered anything but a fringe movement and it has never captured more than a tiny minority of public support. It has received relatively little attention in academia[2] and virtually none in the media or in K-12 schools.

Because it is therefore taken for granted that states must exist, a startling blindness to or denial of the necessary costs of creating and maintaining states has existed. This is true both with respect to existing states and to proto-states, that is, movements that wish to become states. More often, when proto-states clash with each other or with existing states, anarchy is ironically often blamed for the resulting violence and chaos. This is an error as the primary cause of the ensuing violence is the perceived need for each entity to completely vanquish its opponents and drive them out of existence entirely. If any

---

[1] Gustave de Molinari, *The Production of Security* (1849).
[2] But see, Robert Nozick, *Anarchy, State and Utopia* (1974).

3

such disputant in modern times has been anarcho-capitalist in its goals and methods, that is the best kept secret of all time.[3] All known disputants have sought to achieve monopoly state power by defeating all competitors. The sum total of the resulting violence, murder, mayhem, destruction and chaos has been incalculable.

There is no generally accepted word for the gargantuan costs of maintaining or creating states. There is no clear concept for those costs and there has been no comprehensive delineation of those costs. Since we think in concepts and communicate in words, this lacuna means that we have been largely oblivious to the costs of states and proto-states as tied to a concept and as signified by a word that stands for that concept. Since the state system appears to be failing all over the world, this is a serious problem. We propose using the term "archy" to signify such a concept. The term "archy" is descriptive or scientific, *not* normative or judgmental. No moral judgment is necessarily involved in applying the term to any given set of facts. Instead what has happened is that things have been explained, clarified and better understood. People are then free to make whatever moral or value judgments they wish. If you favor archy; if you believe in archism and are proud of its methods and consequences, shout it from the mountaintops. Knock yourselves out.

However, in this book, expect to have the beliefs you may hold in this regard scrutinized and their costs and consequences delineated. And expect certain questions to be posed or intimated that are rarely asked and rarely if ever adequately addressed by archists such as:

1. How do states arise?
2. What should their borders be?
3. What ethnic, racial and religious groups should be included in the state?

---

[3] There was an anarchist movement during the Spanish Civil War that briefly controlled some territory, however, it was the classic left-wing anarchist operation that smuggled in the state but called it a "committee." See, J. Ostrowski, "Chomsky's Economics," *Mises.org*, Jan. 6, 2003.

4

4. Which states are so illegitimate that they should not exist?
5. How do we get rid of bad states?
6. Can parts of states secede and how?

We think that part of the problem with archism is that it begins at the end, considering the need for the existence of the state as self-evident, without establishing its foundations by addressing these questions. Thus, we are in our present predicament. The state system is failing all over the world, yet, virtually no one is questioning that system. We are stuck in the kind of mental trap Einstein alluded to: "We can not solve our problems with the same level of thinking that created them."

So, facing problems that appear to be created by the state system, politicians, stuck in that "same level of thinking," continue to apply the same tool, basically brute force, solving nothing, creating new problems, and all the while being callously oblivious to the consequences. *In their own minds*, they all are just doing their duty or "following orders," while *in reality* they are manufacturing corpses, destroying neighborhoods and cities, devastating cultures, communities and religions and forcing the mass movement of peoples. It is yet another feature of archism that its practitioners can wreak such havoc during the day, doing things that normal human beings not employed by the state consider abhorrent, and sleep like babies at night. Thus, unfortunately, conscience does *not* make cowards of archists.[4]

There is no way that justice can be done in this volume to the long-neglected and complex concepts of archy and archism. However, an important start on such a project has been made and should serve to help illuminate the roots of the disasters in Libya and Syria.

---

[4] *Cf., Hamlet*, Act 3, Scene 1.

1. A Short History of American Intervention in the Middle East

American intervention into the Middle East did not start in Libya and Syria in the last five years. World War I marks the beginning of American involvement in the Middle East. The Ottoman Empire had ruled the Middle East for about 600 years. It is difficult to find evidence the Middle East was a major problem for the United States while it was ruled by the Ottomans.[5]

The first American intervention into the Middle East in modern times comes with American entrance into World War I in 1917 on the side of the Allied Powers including Great Britain and France, the two leading imperial powers of the previous centuries. Ironically, Woodrow Wilson pushed the United States into war to make the world "safe for democracy."[6] During the war, Great Britain, France and Russia agreed on a plan to carve up the post-war Ottoman Empire. The plan was known as the Sykes-Picot plan. This obscure document has suddenly appeared on the news pages as ISIS has vowed to overturn it! Though the United States was not directly involved in drafting the plan, it nonetheless bears some responsibility for its execution, first, because its entrance into the war broke a stalemate and tipped the war towards the Allies, and second, because it acquiesced to the execution of the

---

[5] The exception being the Barbary Wars.
[6] Address to Congress, April 2, 1917.

plan after the war when it was in a position to protest, if not obstruct it.

After the war ended, the Middle East was carved up along the arbitrary lines of the Sykes-Picot plan, resulting in the creation of artificial states filled with ethnic and religious groups hostile to each other. The classic example is Iraq. Iraq is a country consisting of three separate groups with sharply different interests, the Kurds in the North, the Shiites in the South and the Sunnis in the middle. Saddam Hussein kept the lid on the pot with ruthless police state methods. Once he was overthrown by the United States, the country should have been partitioned, but it is official U. S. policy to consider arbitrary boundaries imposed by force on peoples to be sacrosanct. This is part of the syndrome of *archism,* discussed in the Introduction. Suffice it to say here that archism involves the belief that states must be maintained regardless of the costs. As one of the co-authors has explained elsewhere, democracy does not smooth over such sharp multicultural differences but rather exacerbates them.[7] Naturally, the Shiites, constituting about 60 percent of the population, won the post-Saddam elections and began imposing their will on the Sunni minority. A civil war ensued whose chaos ultimately led to the creation of ISIS years later. See Chapter 7.

Syria was yet another artificial state created after World War I by the Western powers. There, the Sunnis were a majority; the Shiites/Alawites were the largest minority and there was a smattering of smaller minorities including Christians. The ancient tensions between the Sunnis and Allawites led to a civil war that once again, gave ISIS the chance to thrive in the chaos and expand its reach.

The United States has been heavily involved with propping up the state of Israel from its creation in 1948 until the present time. President Truman was a wacky individual who dropped a nuclear bomb on a city in 1945, killing women, children and the elderly and called it a "military base."[8] Truman officially recognized Israel against

---

[7] James Ostrowski, *Progressivism: A Primer on the Idea Destroying America* (2014), p. 118.

[8] Radio Report to the American People on the Potsdam Conference (August 9, 1945).

the advice of his Secretary of State, George Marshall, who viewed the move as based on domestic political concerns.[9] Truman did so in large part to ensure the support of American Jews in the upcoming presidential election.[10]

The Palestinians and their Arab allies have nursed a grievance against Israel since 1948 for, in their view, seizing their land by force of arms. We are continually told that Israel is America's most important ally in the Middle East, however, that is the exact opposite of the truth. *America does not need an ally in the Middle East because the United States government does not need to be involved in the Middle East, especially for oil.* Israel, obviously, is a liability to the United States as evidenced by the 9/11 attacks which Osama bin Laden stated, were, directly or indirectly, in part in retaliation for U. S. support for Israel through the years.[11]

Of the two interventions at issue in this book, the Syrian intervention relates directly to American support of Israel. Assad was considered to be a thorn in the side of Israel for many years. There is circumstantial evidence that Clinton's support of Syrian intervention was to appease Israeli interests, generally a smart political move for one whose life-long dream is to be President.

James P. Rubin,[12] a close and long-time associate of Bill and Hillary Clinton, sent an email in April, 2012[13] to Hillary Clinton

---

[9] G. Pops, "Marshall, the Recognition of Israel, and Anti-Semitism," *marshallfoundation.org.*

[10] J. Judis, "Seeds of Doubt," *newrepublic.com,* Jan. 15, 2014.

[11] "Full text: bin Laden's 'letter to America,'" *theguardian.com,* Nov. 24, 2002.

[12] His bio states: "Jamie Rubin served under President Clinton as Assistant Secretary of State and Chief Spokesman for the State Department. He also worked as a top policy advisor to Madeleine Albright during one of America's most challenging periods in foreign relations. Having served on Hillary Clinton's presidential candidate campaign team, Jamie then worked as a policy advisor to the US Secretary of State and to President Obama." jla.co.uk/conference-speakers/james-p-rubin#.V4wvj_krLIV

previewing an article to be published in June in *Foreign Policy* magazine, stating:

> "The best way to help Israel deal with Iran's growing nuclear capability is to help the people of Syria overthrow the regime of Bashar Assad. Negotiations to limit Iran's nuclear program will not solve Israel's security dilemma. . . . At best, the talks between the world's major powers and Iran that began in Istanbul this April and will continue in Baghdad in May will enable Israel to postpone by a few months a decision whether to launch an attack on Iran that could provoke a major Mideast war. *Iran's nuclear program and Syria's civil war may seem unconnected, but they are. . . . What Israeli military leaders really worry about -- but cannot talk about -- is losing their nuclear monopoly.* . . . The result would be a precarious nuclear balance in which Israel could not respond to provocations with conventional military strikes on Syria and Lebanon, as it can today. . . . It is the strategic relationship between Iran and the regime of Bashar Assad in Syria that makes it possible for Iran to undermine Israel's security . . . through its proxies in Lebanon, like Hezbollah, that are sustained, armed and trained by Iran via Syria. The end of the Assad regime would end this dangerous alliance. . . . In short, the White House can ease the tension that has developed with Israel over Iran by doing the right thing in Syria."

Clinton forwarded it on to her aide Monica Hanley.[14] As this email suggests, the Syrian intervention may have been part of a larger chess game involving Israel's main current declared enemy, Iran. As the main Shiite power on earth, Iran is perceived to be an ally of Syria

---

[13] R. Parry, "How Hillary Clinton Ignores Peace," *commondreams.org*, July 2, 2016.

[14] wikileaks.org/clinton-emails/emailid/18061.

and thus, taking down the Shiite-friendly Assad was seen as a way to chip away at Iran's influence.

In a comprehensive review of the failure of American foreign policy in the Middle East, David Stockman writes:

> "The very idea that Tehran is an expansionist power bent on exporting terrorism to the rest of the world is a giant fiction and tissue of lies invented by the Washington War Party and its Bibi Netanyahu branch in order to win political support for their confrontationist policies. Indeed, the three decade long demonization of Iran has served one over-arching purpose. Namely, it enabled both branches of the War Party to conjure up a fearsome enemy, thereby justifying aggressive policies that call for a constant state of war and military mobilization. "[15]

The movement of U. S. foreign policy to demonize and attack Shiite regimes and in the process, ally with Sunni regimes, seems counterintuitive as those Shiite regimes have sponsored or produced very few terrorist attacks against American targets over the years. In sharp contrast, most major terrorist attacks against Americans have been perpetrated by Sunnis.

In return for her Israel First foreign policy, including illegally helping to start a war in Syria in part to help Israel, Hillary Clinton has received and will continue to receive massive material support from pro-Israel donors and PACs.[16]

The bottom line is this. America's foreign intervention in the progressive era, both in Europe and the Middle East itself, has directly or indirectly caused massive problems both for the United States and the Middle East.

---

[15] "Christmas 2015—Why There Is No Peace on Earth," *davidstockmanscontracorner.com*, Dec. 25, 2015.

[16] See, e.g., J. Nathan-Kazis, "Lightning Rod Pro-Hillary Clinton Super PAC Is Mostly Backed by Jewish Donors," *forward.com*, Feb. 13, 2016.

With the interventions into Libya and Syria, we have once again failed to heed George Washington's wise advice, which is notably lacking in progressive sentiments. It is worth quoting at length as each one of his recommendations has been completely ignored in the progressive era of aggressive foreign intervention in the last century or so.

> "[N]othing is more essential than that permanent, inveterate antipathies against particular nations, and passionate attachments for others, should be excluded; and that, in place of them, just and amicable feelings towards all should be cultivated. The nation which indulges towards another a habitual hatred or a habitual fondness is in some degree a slave. It is a slave to its animosity or to its affection, either of which is sufficient to lead it astray from its duty and its interest. Antipathy in one nation against another disposes each more readily to offer insult and injury, to lay hold of slight causes of umbrage, and to be haughty and intractable, when accidental or trifling occasions of dispute occur. Hence, frequent collisions, obstinate, envenomed, and bloody contests. The nation, prompted by ill-will and resentment, sometimes impels to war the government, contrary to the best calculations of policy. The government sometimes participates in the national propensity, and adopts through passion what reason would reject; at other times it makes the animosity of the nation subservient to projects of hostility instigated by pride, ambition, and other sinister and pernicious motives. The peace often, sometimes perhaps the liberty, of nations, has been the victim.
>
> *So likewise, a passionate attachment of one nation for another produces a variety of evils. Sympathy for the favorite nation, facilitating the illusion of an imaginary common interest in cases where no real common interest exists, and infusing into one the enmities of the other, betrays the former into a participation in the*

quarrels and wars of the latter without adequate inducement or justification. It leads also to concessions to the favorite nation of privileges denied to others which is apt doubly to injure the nation making the concessions; by unnecessarily parting with what ought to have been retained, and *by exciting jealousy, ill-will, and a disposition to retaliate, in the parties from whom equal privileges are withheld. . . . The great rule of conduct for us in regard to foreign nations is in extending our commercial relations, to have with them as little political connection as possible. . . . Harmony, liberal intercourse with all nations, are recommended by policy, humanity, and interest."*[17]

---

[17] Farewell Address (1796).

2. Chaos in the Middle East in 2011 and its Culprits

The American interventions into Libya and Syria happened in a troubled part of the world with numerous and seemingly intractable problems that were in many ways the result of prior unwise American foreign policy. This is particularly true with Syria. The Iraq War launched by George Bush in 2003 destabilized the artificial state of Iraq. It is widely recognized that Saddam Hussein was a brutal dictator who held Iraq together and under control by brute force. However, it is rarely acknowledged that, since Iraq is an artificial country created by the Western allies after World War I, it is difficult to conceive of Iraq being held together in any other way than brute force. As one of the co-authors pointed out in 2003, Iraq is made up of three discrete groups with historical and ideological, ethnic and religious differences. The suggestion of peace through partition made in that article was ignored.[18]

Additionally, the elimination of Saddam's secular regime opened the door for various Islamic factions to vie for state power. ISIS emerged out of this power vacuum. Syria, a regime controlled by a Shiite, Bashar al-Assad, was a natural target of ISIS, once it had gained a foothold among its fellow Sunnis in Iraq. Say what you will about ISIS, but they had the savvy to realize what clueless (archist) foreign

---

[18] J. Ostrowski, "Will Iraq Have Democracy or Peace?," *lewrockwell.com*, April 29, 2003.

policy "experts" in the West did not, that the Sykes-Picott borders created by the Western powers were completely arbitrary and bore no relationship to reality in the 21st Century. They ignored them, indeed, explicitly promised to obliterate them.

ISIS did not exist in a self-conscious form in Libya prior to the start of the civil war there in 2011. Rather, that conflict had roots in the Arab Spring. In addition to the wreckage of Iraq, the Arab Spring was the other major development that set the stage for intervention into Libya and Syria.

The Arab Spring is a large and complicated phenomenon that can only be summarized here. What is vital to understand for present purposes is that this conflict was a face-off between the old regime in the Middle East and their opponents, who, whether correctly or not, portrayed themselves as democratic reformers. Which side did the Progressive State of America support? Both sides of course, illustrating the irrational nature of progressivism applied to foreign policy.

The relationship between the United States and Egypt is longstanding. Keep in mind that virtually the entirety of American foreign policy in the Middle East is based on the simple concept of Israel First.[19] That is, the United States does what Israel and its allies *think* is in the best interest of Israel. Of course, it can never be called what it is, Israel First. Rather, it is always sold to the gullible American public as necessary to fight terrorism or to keep the oil flowing.

Both rationalizations are nonsense of course. In fact, both propositions are the precise opposite of the truth. The only obstacle to the free flow of oil is America's numerous, prior and unwise interventions into the Middle East directly or indirectly on behalf of Israel. David Stockman traces this pernicious fallacy to Henry Kissinger: "That doctrine has been wrong from the day it was officially enunciated by one of America's great economic ignoramuses, Henry Kissinger, at the time of the original oil crisis in 1973. The 42 years since then have proven in spades that it doesn't matter who controls

---

[19] If that led to the cover up of an Israeli attack on the United States Navy ship U. S. S. Liberty in 1967, so be it.

the oilfields, and that the only effective cure for high oil prices is the free market."[20]

Likewise, America has been attacked by terrorists largely because of its prior unwise interventions on behalf of Israel. These facts are really not debatable by any honest observer. Rather, those blinded by self-interest or ideology are in denial about these facts and respond by shooting the messenger.

Thus, America's relationship with Egypt is largely a function of its slavish devotion to Israel. Egypt made peace with Israel in 1979. Naturally, America must bribe Egypt to pretend to like Israel. That mandate led the United States to subsidize the brutal dictatorship of Hosni Mubarak from 1979 through 2011. Mubarak's regime featured systematic torture, massive violations of free speech and assembly, interference with elections and persecution of gays.[21] All the while, this evil regime was propped up by Uncle Sam. The only sin Egypt avoided was attacking Israel. The Feds mulcted about two billion dollars a year from the U. S. taxpayer to bribe Egypt and its corrupt power elite.[22] Officially, the aid was "unconditional." Unofficially, there was the one condition previously stated.

It is worth noting that one of the reasons bin Laden gave for the 9/11 attacks was U. S. support for Egypt.[23]

Thus, decades of oppression from the U.S.-backed Mubarak regime led to an uprising in Egypt. But the U. S. backed Mubarak's *opponents* as well. The New York Times reported in 2011 that:

> "a small core of American government-financed organizations were promoting democracy in authoritarian Arab states. . . . the United States' democracy-building campaigns played a bigger role in fomenting protests than was previously known, with

---

[20] D. Stockman, *supra.*

[21] E. Loftis, "Mubarak's Horrific Human Rights Legacy," *motherjones.com*, 2/1/11.

[22] T. Meyer, "F.A.Q. on U.S. Aid to Egypt: Where Does the Money Go, And How Is It Spent?," *propublica.org*, 10/9/13.

[23] "Full text: bin Laden's 'letter to America,'" *supra.*

key leaders of the movements having been trained by the Americans in campaigning, organizing through new media tools and monitoring elections."[24]

Thus, the Progressive State of America was supporting both sides in the Arab Spring uprising that eventually spread to Libya and set the stage for the disastrous American intervention there that is the subject of this book and which, along with the Syrian catastrophe, has the world flirting with disaster.

---

[24] R. Nixon, "U.S. Groups Helped Nurture Arab Uprisings," *nytimes.com*, April 14, 2011.

3. The Illegal American Invasion of Libya

On March 19th, 2011 President Barack Hussein Obama lost whatever was left of his reputation as a man of peace. He was awarded a Nobel Peace Prize in what may have been the first such award based on hope as opposed to the historical record. Those hopes were dashed when the United States attacked Libya under the guise of a NATO operation, though the brains and drive behind the scenes was largely U. S.-based. The President's blunder helped pave the way for ISIS, which had been little more than a loose band of latter day Barbary pirates. This illegal war made possible the spread of that elusive jihadist fantasy, restoration of the Caliphate. The president's point person for this invasion, Secretary of State Hillary Rodham Clinton, has her fingerprints all over this blunder as evidenced by her now notorious post-Gaddafi murder statement: "We came, we saw, he died."[25]

Muammar Gaddafi had been raising hell in Northern Africa for decades. If the standard for regime change NATO and the UN applied to the late Colonel Gaddafi, was applied worldwide, dozens of world leaders would have to get their affairs in order. The real motives of this illegal invasion should be thoroughly investigated by the U. S. House of Representatives and the guilty parties punished in proportion to the damage caused by the invasion.

Lies and war are very close relatives. Those who favor war, that is, the planned and systematic destruction of people and property with the intention of imposing one's will on the survivors, would not

---

[25] https://www.youtube.com/watch?v=Fgcd1ghag5Y.

hesitate for a second to lie their way into war. This follows as a matter of logic as war—getting what you want by killing—is a greater evil than lying—getting what you want by trickery, since the victim of the lie at least remains alive.

Looking at the history of American wars since and including the Civil War (that term being a lie in itself); it is harder to think of the genesis of a war that did not involve lies than it is to think of one that did. "Remember the Maine," Wilson's, FDR's and LBJ's promises to stay out of war,[26] the Gulf of Tonkin and "weapons of mass destruction" come to mind. The American intervention into Libya was no exception. Lies, half-truths and critical omissions served to pave the way toward intervention and to disguise the usual panoply of hidden agendas.[27] The war on truth, designed to overcome the will of the people at home, precedes and facilitates the war on people and property abroad to come.

The American intervention into Libya was sold primarily as a means to prevent Gaddafi from committing genocide against his own people. President Obama said on national television on March 28, 2011:

> "We knew that if we wanted -- if we waited one more day, Benghazi, a city nearly the size of Charlotte, could suffer a massacre that would have reverberated across the region and stained the conscience of the world. It was not in our national interest to let that happen. I refused to let that happen. And so nine days ago, after consulting the bipartisan leadership of Congress,

---

[26] See, R. Higgs, "To Make War, Presidents Lie," *theindependent.org*, Oct. 1, 2002. Wilson's slogan in 1916 was "He kept us out of war." FDR said, "Your boys are not going to be sent into any foreign wars." LBJ said, We are not about to send American boys 9 or 10,000 miles away from home to do what Asian boys ought to be doing for themselves."

[27] An April, 2011 email sent to Clinton by Sidney Blumenthal outlines several such possible hidden agendas involving the French including oil, imperialism, domestic political considerations and even gold.

I authorized military action to stop the killing and enforce U.N. Security Council Resolution 1973."

Before we get into the truth of that assertion, it is worth noting that here, the President makes it clear that he has zero regard for the Constitutional limits of his war powers. Instead, he substitutes his own judgment as to what is in the "national interest." A careful reading of the Obama Doctrine indicates that Obama believes that any time there is a revolt against an authoritarian state by a group that *Obama thinks*, against all available evidence, might be democratic, it is the duty of the United States, without Congressional approval, to intervene on the side of the rebels if the dictator has the temerity to fight back. This of course makes the United States the declared enemy of all authoritarian regimes. These regimes then have an incentive to create a nuclear capacity to scare off Uncle Sam. It also makes the U. S. military and treasury the plaything of any rag tag group of rebels that is able to sweet talk Administration officials into thinking they will install a Western-style democracy after they seize power by brute force.

Granted that the Obama Doctrine is absurd, dangerous and unconstitutional, but did Obama, Clinton and their allies tell the truth in this particular instance? No. Congressman Peter Hoekstra, in his 2015 book, *Architects of Disaster: The Destruction of Libya*, has delineated the numerous lies, distortions and half-truths used to justify intervention:

- The death toll from the war was "greatly inflated." Figures as high as 50,000 were widely reported, however, the actual numbers were closer to 4700 dead and 2100 missing according to Hoekstra, Chairman of the House Intelligence Committee for many years.
- It was falsely alleged that Gaddafi used "armed helicopters to butcher unarmed demonstrators."
- There were false allegations of mass rapes by Gaddafi's forces.

21

- It was falsely claimed that "Gaddafi was employing thousands of mercenaries from sub-Saharan countries to kill protesters."

Nor was Obama's claim of an imminent "massacre" or Clinton's prediction of a "slaughter" supported by the facts. An investigation by the Washington Times concluded:

> "The intelligence community had few facts to back up Mrs. Clinton's audacious predictions, officials told The Times. In fact, the Pentagon's judgment was that Gadhafi was unlikely to risk world outrage by inflicting large civilian casualties as he cracked down on the rebels based in Benghazi, the officials said. Some accounts said the Libyan forces were attacking unarmed protesters, but no genocide was reported, the officials said. . . . Furthermore, defense officials had direct information from their intelligence asset in contact with the regime that Gadhafi gave specific orders not to attack civilians and to narrowly focus the war on the armed rebels, according to the asset, who survived the war. All spoke to The Times on the condition of anonymity but confirmed Col. Gadhafi's order."[28]

Yet another major act of deception was the mischaracterization of the rebels as would-be democratic pioneers. In fact, the Administration knew or should have known that the bulk of the

---

[28] K. Riddell & J. Shapiro, "Hillary Clinton's 'WMD' moment: U.S. intelligence saw false narrative in Libya," *washingtontimes.com*, Jan. 29, 2015; see also, A. Kuperman, "Obama's Libya Debacle," *foreignaffairs.com*, March/April 2015. "There is no evidence or reason to believe that Qaddafi had planned or intended to perpetuate a killing campaign."

rebels were jihadists whose vision of a new regime was far worse than the reality of Gaddafi's.[29]

The nature of the American intervention was itself the subject of deception. The UN resolution, which was the alleged basis for American involvement was, according to Hillary Clinton, "to enforce the no-fly zone and protect civilians in Libya."[30] However, the mission actually became, and was probably always intended to be rather different: regime change.[31] As Micah Zenko wrote, "given that decapitation strikes against Gaddafi were employed early and often, there almost certainly was a decision by the civilian heads of government and the NATO coalition to 'take him out' from the very beginning of the intervention."[32] Zenko also believes that the Americans and their allies not only exceeded the scope of their mandate but actually *violated it* by arming the rebels: "Egypt and Qatar were shipping advanced weapons to rebel groups the whole time, with the blessing of the Obama administration, while Western intelligence and military forces provided battlefield intelligence, logistics, and training support." Zenko also cites a video released by NATO itself which shows a Canadian frigate allowing a rebel tugboat loaded with banned weapons and explosives to proceed on its way unmolested.[33] Zenko concludes:

> "In truth, the Libyan intervention was about regime change from the very start. The threat posed by the Libyan regime's military and paramilitary forces to civilian-populated areas was diminished by NATO airstrikes and rebel ground movements within the first 10 days. Afterward, NATO began providing direct

---

[29] With respect to the Syrian rebels, see G. Abdul-Ahad, "Al-Qaida turns tide for rebels in battle for eastern Syria," *theguardian.com*, July 30, 2012.

[30] Hillary Clinton, *Hard Choices*.

[31] M. Zenko, "The Big Lie about the Libyan War," *ForeignPolicy.com* (Mar. 22, 2016); A. Kuperman, *supra*.

[32] *Id.*

[33] *Id.*

close-air support for advancing rebel forces by attacking government troops that were actually in retreat and had abandoned their vehicles. Fittingly, on Oct. 20, 2011, it was a U.S. Predator drone and French fighter aircraft that attacked a convoy of regime loyalists trying to flee Qaddafi's hometown of Sirte. The dictator was injured in the attack, captured alive, and then extrajudicially murdered by rebel forces."[34]

Thus, the Libyan intervention was an unlawful and unwise act of war, essentially an invasion of a country that had not attacked the United States. The intervention was sold by the usual panoply of lies, distortions and half-truths. There was no plan or possibility of a plan for the creation of a better regime after the invasion. In fact, all the available evidence indicated that Libya would turn into a nightmare after Gaddafi was deposed. That is exactly what happened.

---

[34] *Id.*

24

4. The Consequences for Libya

It appears likely that the allegations against Gaddafi were at least exaggerated to justify the invasion. If these charges were intentionally made up to murder a head of state in a prosperous nation in Africa, impeachment is the least of the problems awaiting Barack Obama and Hillary Clinton. In assessing the damage done to Libya from this violent intervention, let's take a chronological look at the ensuing five years from the firing of the first missile.

Before the civil war, Libya, although far from perfect, was a stable and relatively wealthy country in a part of the world where neither element is common. Today, Libya is in a state of chaos and civil war.[35] There are competing governments, which contrary to popular belief, is attributable to *archy*, not *anarchy*.[36] After seven months of bombing, "downtown Benghazi is in ruins" and parts of the city are under the control of a militia deemed a terrorist organization by the United States.[37] Ben Norton sums up the damage:

> "As for the rest of Libya, much of the land is now controlled by rival warlords.. . . No end is in sight for

---

[35] B. Norton, "The Trey Gowdy/Hillary Clinton Conspiracy: The Real Benghazi Scandal Only Chairman Noam Chomsky Would Uncover," *Salon.com*, Oct. 26, 2015.

[36] See the Introduction; A. Kuperman, *supra*.

[37] *Id.*

Libya's civil war, which has already dragged on for many months, leaving thousands of people dead. Because chaos reigns in large swaths of the country, there is no official figure for the deaths. The project Libya Body Count, which simply compiles media reports, and is thus conservative in its estimates, has documented over 4,000 fatalities since 2014. This violent chaos has furthermore sparked a flood of refugees, exacerbating what is already the worst refugee crisis since World War II. Hundreds of thousands of Libyan civilians have been forced to flee, often on dangerous smuggling boats. As of December 2014, the U.N. estimated there were over 370,000 displaced Libyans. The number is likely higher today, a year later. . . . Benghazi . . . remains roiled in violence. In the words of AP, the city is 'shattered.'"[38]

Seumas Milne, writing for the Guardian, adds that 8000 prisoners have been held without trial and noted "rampant torture and routine deaths in detention" and the ethnic cleansing and persecution of black Libyans.[39] Alan Kuperman adds: "As bad as Libya's human rights situation was under Qaddafi, it has gotten worse since NATO ousted him. Immediately after taking power, the rebels perpetrated scores of reprisal killings, in addition to torturing, beating, and arbitrarily detaining thousands of suspected Qaddafi supporters. * * * NATO's intervention appears to have increased the violent death toll more than tenfold."[40]

Contrary to the incredibly naïve fantasies of Obama and Clinton, Libya, "freed" from Gadaffi, has not turned into a New England-style town meeting democracy, but has descended into a multi-party civil

---

[38] *Id.*

[39] "If there were global justice, NATO would be in the dock over Libya," May 15, 2012.

[40] A. Kuperman, *supra.*

war of all against all, a war that is beginning to spill over into neighboring Tunisia.[41]

A lengthy report by the New York Times concluded that:

> "The looting of Colonel Qaddafi's vast weapons arsenals during the intervention has fed the Syrian civil war, empowered terrorist and criminal groups from Nigeria to Sinai, and destabilized Mali, where Islamist militants stormed a Radisson hotel in November and killed 20 people.
>
> "A growing trade in humans has sent a quarter-million refugees north across the Mediterranean, with hundreds drowning en route. A civil war in Libya has left the country with two rival governments, cities in ruins and more than 4,000 dead."[42]

The nightmare produced by the Obama/Clinton regime change reached its denouement in February of 2015, on Libyan soil, when ISIS executed 21 Coptic Christians for nothing more than being Christian. This barbaric act occurred less than four years after the "successful" invasion authored by Barack Obama and Hillary Clinton. These progressive politicians helped create a safe space for ISIS, a new killing field. Obama and Clinton have the blood of tens of thousands on their hands.

Justin Raimondo, editor of Antiwar.com, wrote:

> "A woman who could very well occupy the highest office in the land, with near total control of US foreign policy, basically committed an entire nation to

---

[41] F. Samti & D. Walsh, "Tunisian Clash Spreads Fear That Libyan War Is Spilling Over," *NewYorkTimes.com*, Mar. 7, 2016.
[42] J. Becker & S. Shane, "Hillary Clinton, 'Smart Power' and a Dictator's Fall," *nytimes.com*, Feb. 27, 2016.

perdition. Where's the outrage? Who is drawing the lessons learned from all this?"[43]

---

[43] "Libya: How Hillary Clinton Destroyed a Country," *Antiwar.com*, March 4, 2016.

5. The Illegal American Intervention into Syria

The election of Barack Obama brought a promise of peace to a nation that had been at war since 2001. Yet, new wars were conjured up to replace the ones that were winding down. Not content with the mess they had created in Libya, Obama and Clinton were busy planning the next war to make the world safe for democracy, Syria. To understand the nature of Obama's "second war", it is essential to review a brilliant article that ties together the various loose ends of Obama's second illegal war. Seymour Hersh's "The Rat Line And The Red Line" expertly explains the trickery of Obama's and Hillary's machinations:

> "The full extent of US co-operation with Turkey, Saudi Arabia and Qatar in assisting the rebel opposition in Syria has yet to come to light. The Obama administration has never publicly admitted to its role in creating what the CIA calls a 'rat line', a back channel highway into Syria. The rat line, authorized in early 2012, was used to funnel weapons and ammunition from Libya via southern Turkey and across the Syrian border to the opposition. Many of those in Syria who ultimately received the weapons were jihadists, some of them affiliated with al-Qaida. . . .

"A highly classified annex to the [Senate Intelligence Committee report on Bengazi], not made public, described a secret agreement reached in early 2012 between the Obama and Erdoğan administrations. It pertained to the rat line. By the terms of the agreement, funding came from Turkey, as well as Saudi Arabia and Qatar; the CIA, with the support of MI6, was responsible for getting arms from Gaddafi's arsenals into Syria."[44]

Apparently, Obama was persuaded by Turkey and Saudi Arabia to arm Jihadi rebels in Syria with the murdered Gaddafi's weapons cache, which served to bring a NATO ally, Turkey close to a serious war with a nuclear power, Russia. This danger persists today. This ill-informed group worked with Turkey, a NATO ally in essentially arming ISIS in Syria. Such a foreign policy blunder presently has the world on edge concerning Russia and Turkey's serious game of chicken, caused by the illegal wars in Libya and Syria overseen by Obama and Clinton.

* * * * *

For thousands of years, Syria has been located in a very tough neighborhood.[45] The notion of limited government, natural human rights, tolerance of minorities, due process, the rights of the accused and freedom of speech have barely made a dent in politics there. Authoritarian regimes or dictatorships have ruled Syria for many centuries, and, barring a sudden conversion to classical liberalism by the masses that live there, such a regime is likely to persist for years to

---

[44] S. Hersh, "The Red Line and the Rat Line," *London Review of Books*, April 17, 2014; see also, D. McElroy, "CIA 'running arms smuggling team in Benghazi when consulate was attacked,'" *telegraph.co.uk*, Aug. 2, 2013; D. Griffin & K. Johnston, "Exclusive: Dozens of CIA operatives on the ground during Benghazi attack," *cnn.com*, Aug. 1, 2013; A. Newman, *supra*.

[45] See, "A History Behind Syrian Civil War," BBC Documentary, *vimeo.com*/73922135.

come. In Syria, toppling one regime means its replacement by a similar one and possibly worse. Into this hard reality came, in the last few years, naïve progressives from the West who thought they could impose a better regime on the country by force, while making no changes in the culture or the people.

Such foolishness is typical of progressives, indeed, inevitable given that progressivism is not a rational or fact-based system of thought but a form of infantile wishful thinking. A classic instance of this "thinking" is Hillary Clinton's statement about Syria: "We urgently seek solutions, however hard they are to find."[46] Along the same lines are her slogan that, in the choice between action and inaction, she wants to be "caught trying" and her "deep belief in American power to do good."[47] The underlying premise, utterly lacking any rational basis, is that there is a governmental, that is, coercive, solution for any given problem. Never considered in this ideology, is whether governmental action caused the problem in the first place!

For decades, Syria has been ruled by the country's Alawite/Shiite religious minority, a group nursing ancient grievances against the Sunni majority and with fresh memories of an atrocity that occurred in the 14th Century.[48] Even Alawite critics of the regime conceded widespread fear of Sunni reprisals if the regime is overthrown.[49] "We all know that the Sunnis offered the Alawites nothing but death and threats," one Alawite religious leader stated. "The Alawites' history is 1,000 years of persecution. The Sunnis intend to continue with this."[50] Given these facts, it should have been obvious to any intelligence service that any effort to overthrow the regime would be costly, vicious and bloody. It was and is. The only way out of this predicament was to guarantee all minority rights if the regime fell and this was not done. Nor was it possible to accomplish anyway.

---

[46] R. Sterling, "The Wicked War on Syria: Hillary Clinton in Her Own Words," *counterpunch.org*, Sept. 30, 2015.
[47] J. Becker & S. Shane, *supra*.
[48] See, "A History Behind Syrian Civil War," *supra*.
[49] R. Spencer, "Leaders of Syrian Alawite sect threaten to abandon Bashar al-Assad," *The Telegraph*, April 3, 2016.
[50] *Id.*

This is the context within which the American government, under the leadership of Barack Obama and Hillary Clinton, and without any legal or constitutional authority, aided efforts to overthrow the Syrian regime.

A variety of sources indicate that the CIA provided training and material assistance to the rebels fighting to overthrow the Assad regime in Syria.[51] What is yet to be determined is the precise timelines of the intervention. This is critical as Hillary Clinton left office on February 1, 2013. However, it has also been alleged that she continued to be "consulted" about program.[52] It is also reported that she urged Obama to intervene in Syria before he actually did so.[53]

One of the earliest reports of American involvement in Syria was published by the New York Times on June 21, 2012, well before Clinton left office. The involvement was limited, however, to vetting which rebel groups got weapons.[54] A later published article, however, reports on significant American involvement in Syria well before Clinton left office:

> "With help from the C.I.A., Arab governments and Turkey have sharply increased their military aid to Syria's opposition fighters in recent months, expanding a secret airlift of arms and equipment for the uprising against President Bashar al Assad, according to air traffic data, interviews with officials in several countries and the accounts of rebel commanders. The airlift, which began on a small scale in early 2012 and continued intermittently through last fall, expanded into a steady and much heavier flow late last year, the data shows. . . . And even as the Obama administration

---

[51] A. Johnson, "Down the Memory Hole: NYT Erases CIA's Efforts to Overthrow Syria's Government," *commondreams.org*, Sept. 21, 2015.
[52] R. Sterling, *supra*.
[53] M. Landler, "How Hillary Clinton Became a Hawk," *nytimes.com*, April 21, 2016.
[54] E. Schmitt, "C.I.A. Said to Aid in Steering Arms to Syrian Opposition," *nytimes.com*.

has publicly refused to give more than "nonlethal" aid to the rebels, the involvement of the C.I.A. in the arms shipments — albeit mostly in a consultative role, American officials say — has shown that the United States is more willing to help its Arab allies support the lethal side of the civil war. . . . The former American official said David H. Petraeus, the C.I.A. director until November, had been instrumental in helping to get this aviation network moving and had prodded various countries to work together on it."[55]

Significantly, Clinton and Petraeus appeared to have a close working relationship with respect to Syria. In another report, which both shows Clinton's support for Syrian intervention but could also be used to mitigate her role, the *New York Times* stated that a Clinton/Petraeus plan to arm Syrian rebels was rejected by Obama.[56] That being the case, the timeline of Hillary Clinton's involvement in the Syrian operation is a key issue that requires further investigation by the House of Representatives.

The investigation would likely start with Clinton's own words in her book *Hard Choices* (2014). There, she admits to meeting with several Arab governments in March, 2012 and was urged to "get arms to the rebels." While denying the United States was arming rebels, she boasts of providing so-called humanitarian assistance to the rebels such as pickup trucks, computers, telephones and food rations. Arguably, however, any material aid to a combatant known to be used in hostilities can be considered an act of war in international law.

As for the kind of military aid that Clinton denied was occurring, according to Adam Johnson, the "program . . . trained approximately 10,000 rebel fighters at a cost of $1 billion a year, or roughly 1/15th of the CIA's official annual budget."[57] Seymour Hersh writes that the

---

[55] C. Chivers & E. Schmitt, "Arms Airlift to Syria Rebels Expands, With Aid From C.I.A.," *nytimes.com*, March 24, 2013.
[56] M. Gordon & M. Landler, "Backstage Glimpses of Clinton as Dogged Diplomat, Win or Lose," *nytimes.com*, Feb. 2, 2013.
[57] *Id.*

assistance was "authorized in early 2012, was used to funnel weapons and ammunition from Libya via southern Turkey and across the Syrian border to the opposition. Many of those in Syria who ultimately received the weapons were jihadists, some of them affiliated with al-Qaida. (The DNI spokesperson said: 'The idea that the United States was providing weapons from Libya to anyone is false.')"[58]

Hersh reports that David Petraeus ran the operation and that the gun-running involved the consulate in Benghazi, later attacked by terrorists on September 11, 2012.[59] The New York Times recently reported that a separate but related program to funnel arms through Jordan to Syria was commenced in April 2013.[60] These programs are separate from a failed effort by the Pentagon to arm "moderates."[61] Yet another report places the Jordanian program earlier in the calendar, around the summer of 2012.[62]

While there are credible allegations of American intervention after the outbreak of hostilities, it is not clear how deep the rabbit hole goes. That is, those who justify American intervention argue that Assad used excessive force in quelling protests against his regime. Did, however, the U. S. regime stir up such protests in the first place and create the rationale for the regime change it was plotting from the beginning? A new book suggests this was the case. The prominent libertarian blog, *TargetLiberty.com* recently reported that in a new book, undercover CIA operative Douglas Laux admitted "being part of a top secret task force involved with instigating the Syrian Civil War."[63] The title of the book is *Left of Boom: How a Young CIA Case Officer Penetrated the Taliban and Al-*

---

[58] "The Red Line and the Rat Line," *London Review of Books*, April 17, 2014.

[59] *Id.*

[60] M. Mazzetti, "C.I.A. Arms for Syrian Rebels Supplied Black Market, Officials Say," *nytimes.com*, June 26, 2016.

[61] *Id.*

[62] J. Borger & N. Hopkins, "West training Syrian rebels in Jordan," *theguardian.com*, March 8, 2013.

[63] *TargetLiberty.com*, April 14, 2016 (reprinted with permission of Target Liberty and Daniel McAdams); see also, C. Skelton, "The Syrian opposition: who's doing the talking," *theguardian.com*, July 12, 2012.

Qaeda. *Target Liberty* notes that the description of the book on Amazon states:

> "Douglas Laux is a former CIA operations officer who served multiple tours throughout the Middle East. He was in Afghanistan for the 2010 Afghan Surge, and in Kandahar during Operation Neptune Spear, which resulted in the death of Usama bin Ladin. His final assignment was with the top secret task force involved with instigating the Syrian civil war."

According to Target Liberty, "This is the first public admission by anyone involved with the US government that the US had a role in starting the Syrian civil war. Up to this point, it was only a Wikileaks cable that suggested such an operation might have taken place." As Target Liberty reports, "Daniel McAdams, executive director of the Ron Paul Institute for Peace and Prosperity, recognized the significance of the leaked cable and reported on it at the time of the leak last September." McAdams wrote:

> "The US government has been relying on its standard narrative that the Syria crisis emerged spontaneously after an "Arab Spring" inspired protest was violently suppressed by the Syrian government. The entire US intervention was justified on these grounds. Thus the Obama Administration, as it did in Ukraine, has attempted to disavow any role in fomenting the uprising and thus any responsibility for the violence that ensued.

> "But like much else in US foreign policy the narrative is wholly false, constructed to propagandize the American people in favor of US intervention and shield the US government from any fallout.

> "In fact the US government had long had its sights on regime change in Syria, starting at least with the Project

for a New American Century's plan peddled to George W. Bush to overthrow five countries in five years and remake the entire Middle East. The neocons always like to think big, but like any slimy salesman they never deliver as promised. Their Iraq 'cakewalk' proved a death walk.

"In 2006, according to a secret State Department cable made public by Wikileaks, US Embassy Damascus drafted an extensive memo outlining nine 'vulnerabilities' of the Syrian government with corresponding 'possible actions' on how the US can exploit these 'vulnerabilities' to destabilize the government of Syria.

"The State Department cable was authored by William V. Roebuck, who was at the time the Political Counselor at the US Embassy in Damascus. Roebuck has since been rewarded for his 'good work' on destabilizing Syria and now serves as US Ambassador to Bahrain, where one presumes his role is rather the opposite of what it was in Syria.

"Roebuck's bio suggests he has been somewhat of a regime change rock star: He managed the fallout from US regime change operations in Egypt, Libya, and Iraq, with a stint at the US Embassy in Israel as well.

"What did Roebuck advise the US to do to Syria in 2006? Exploit the Syrian government's fight against Islamist extremists in an attempt to undermine Assad's position in the region.

"That's right: use Syria's fight against al-Qaeda against it. Perhaps it's best to let Roebuck speak for himself. The Syrian government's "vulnerability" is:

'Extremist elements increasingly use Syria as a base, while the SARG (ed: Syrian government) has taken some actions against groups stating links to Al-Qaeda. With the killing of the al-Qaida leader on the border with Lebanon in early December and the increasing terrorist attacks inside Syria culminating in the September 12 attack against the US embassy, the SARG's policies in Iraq and support for terrorists elsewhere as well can be seen to be coming home to roost.'

"How to exploit that vulnerability? In Roebuck's own words:

'Possible Actions: -- Publicize presence of transiting (or externally focused) extremist groups in Syria, not limited to mention of Hamas and PIJ. Publicize Syrian efforts against extremist groups in a way that suggests weakness, signs of instability, and uncontrolled blowback. The SARG,s argument (usually used after terror attacks in Syria) that it too is a victim of terrorism should be used against it to give greater prominence to increasing signs of instability within Syria. (emphasis added).'

"The US had long planned to overthrow Assad well before 2011 and had obviously spent a great deal of time, effort, and money cooking up plans to exploit whatever "vulnerabilities" he may have had to help make that overthrow happen. Roebuck captures that essence in the summary of his 2006 US Embassy Damascus secret cable:

'The bottom line is that Bashar is entering the new year in a stronger position than he has been in several years, but those strengths also carry with them -- or sometimes mask -- vulnerabilities. If we are ready to capitalize, they will offer us opportunities to disrupt his decision-making, keep him off-balance, and make him pay a premium for his mistakes.'

'"If we are ready to capitalize...'

"Yes, they were ready to capitalize. And more than 200,000 people have been killed as the US 'capitalized' on vulnerabilities produced by Assad's fight against terrorists unleashed on his country by the US attack on Iraq. At this point, US foreign policy toward Syria has become too grotesque to even contemplate. In another time there would be a Nuremberg readying the dock for Roebuck and anyone else associated with this mass murder. These days the media just keeps churning out a steady diet of US regime propaganda."

Target Liberty's editor, Robert Wenzel, concludes:

"The Laux disclosure confirms the analysis of McAdams that the Syria crisis did not emerge spontaneously after an "Arab Spring" inspired protest was violently suppressed by the Syrian government. As Laux admits, there was a top secret US operation to instigate the civil war in Syria."

Thus, as with Libya, it appears that Obama and Clinton, working together but not fully disclosing their activities and sometimes denying them, chose to aid and arm rebels seeking to overthrow the Syrian government. Their efforts were not as open, obvious and consequential as they were in Libya. However, it must be assumed that such significant efforts, involving large sums of money and logistical support, had a measurable impact on the civil war, both lengthening it and intensifying it. All of this was done without the slightest hint of legal justification. There was no declaration of war by Congress,[64] no imminent attack on the United States and not even the fig leaf of a United Nations resolution. The result has been a disaster as it was in Libya. How much of the disaster is attributable to the actions of Obama and Clinton can be debated and surely their lawyers in any impeachment hearing will argue their incompetence and impotence in the matter as a defense.

---

[64] Congress did authorize an effort against ISIS on September 17, 2014. See, "Statement By the President on Congressional Authorization to Train Syrian Opposition," Sept. 18, 2014.

6. The Consequences for Syria

Syria is in even worse shape than Libya. It has suffered through five years of brutal multi-party civil war with intervention from major powers and sometimes one of the major powers backing two factions fighting each other.[65] Atrocities and war crimes abound. In these times and in that region, Christian just war theory simply does not apply. Estimates of casualties vary widely but we can assume at least 100,000 have died in the conflict.[66] Injuries must be a multiple of that and physical destruction is in the billions. Infectious disease is spreading due to the damage to infrastructure.[67] Horrendous living conditions have led hundreds of thousands of refugees to flee as discussed in Chapter 8. Alan Kuperman summarizes the costs: "the consequence has been the tragic exacerbation of three pathologies: humanitarian suffering, sectarianism, and radical Islam."[68]

ISIS, which grew as a result of the bone-headed invasions of Libya and Syria co-authored by Barack Obama and Hillary Clinton, has ransacked its way across the region, stealing, torturing, raping and murdering any and all who get in their way. Not only "infidels," but Shiites are victimized.

---

[65] N. Bulos, W. Hennigan & B. Bennett, "In Syria, militias armed by the Pentagon fight those armed by the CIA," *latimes.com*, March 27, 2016.

[66] See, wikipedia.org/wiki/Casualties_of_the_Syrian_Civil_War.

[67] S. Sharara and S. Kanj, "War and Infectious Diseases: Challenges of the Syrian Civil War," *PLoS Pathog.* 2014 Nov. 10(11).

[68] A. Kuperman, *supra*.

Jeffrey Sachs sums up the debacle nicely:

> "The U.S. policy was a massive, horrific failure. Assad did not go, and was not defeated. Russia came to his support. Iran came to his support. The mercenaries sent in to overthrow him were themselves radical jihadists with their own agendas. The chaos opened the way for the Islamic State, building on disaffected Iraqi Army leaders (deposed by the US in 2003), on captured U.S. weaponry, and on the considerable backing by Saudi funds. If the truth were fully known, the multiple scandals involved would surely rival Watergate in shaking the foundations of the US establishment."[69]

What is not clear is precisely how much of the murder and mayhem is traceable to the intervention of the United States. Did that intervention precede and cause the civil war or come later and merely exacerbate the situation? A Congressional investigation is needed to resolve those issues.

The one big promise the state system and its ideology, archism, make is *order* but all these competing states and proto-states have produced is chaos, violence and disorder. Worse yet, they learn nothing; their mindset never changes and they continue to use the same strategies, methodologies and tactics that have failed them so far. They do not and will not, as our late father[70] often advised when we acted up, "meditate on the virtues of peace."

---

[69] "Hillary Clinton and the Syrian Bloodbath," *huffingtonpost.com*, Feb. 14, 2016.

[70] William J. Ostrowski (1925-2011), a lawyer, judge and hero of World War II.

7. The Creation of ISIS

Though there are differing views as to how ISIS was created, the powerful entity known as ISIS barely had a pulse the day of the invasion of Libya authored by President Obama and Hillary Clinton. In less than five years ISIS has emerged as perhaps the world's most ominous threat. It is easy to see then that ISIS metastasized after the invasions of Libya and Syria.

The general philosophy of ISIS originated with the extreme branch of Sunni Wahhabism promoted and funded by The House of Saud. This first came to public attention through Osama bin Laden. An even more radical version was developed by Abu Musab al Zarqawi. However, what gave ISIS room and impetus to grow were the illegal interventions into Libya and Syria by President Obama and Hillary Clinton. They allowed ISIS to morph into the worldwide threat it is today.

There is no dispute that ISIS evolved from al Qaeda, which in turn was inspired by the Wahabbi branch of Islam associated with the House of Saud. This Sunni branch of extreme radical Islam has as its goal the creation of a worldwide Caliphate. This seemingly insane movement would have been and was, laughed at by many intellectuals worldwide a few years back. The recent Paris assassinations and other terrorist attacks have these individuals thinking twice. Would you casually accept a free round trip airline ticket to the Middle East? The world is presently in a profound crisis. How did we get to this dangerous condition?

No doubt the longtime U. S. intervention in the Middle East has contributed to the rise of various radical Islamist groups. Many leftist writers and analysts blame the Iraq invasion and subsequent war which Hillary Clinton supported. However, the rapid growth of ISIS was also facilitated by the later policy blunders of Obama and Clinton.

The undisputed creator of ISIS, Abu Musab al-Zarqawi was killed in a U. S. air strike in Jordan on June 7th, 2006. At that point his fledgling, "al Qaeda on crack" movement had fallen into decline. Two short years later a promising figure rose from virtually nowhere, made America feel good again after a rough period and was resoundingly elected president. Less than five years after ISIS's creator was killed in a US airstrike, the Middle East was suddenly enveloped by a hopeful phenomenon known as the Arab Spring, where common Arab citizens would rise up against their cruel oppressors. The new Obama administration was not going to let a seemingly perfect opportunity go to waste. The sympathetic Obama White House teamed up with NATO to quicken this movement across the Middle East in an effort to utopianize Islam.

Their original huckleberry would be the unsympathetic Muammar Gaddafi. The anti-Gaddafi propaganda was intensified and on March 11th, 2011 NATO forces invaded Libya. Just a few months later, Gaddafi was murdered in gruesome fashion. The most important point concerning the size and scope of ISIS is that less than five years after the death of Abu Musab al-Zarqawi, his ISIS brigades had deteriorated into a small force on the day NATO/US invaded Libya.

The CIA estimated in 2014 that ISIS had about 25,000 fighters.[71] However, a more realistic estimate was made by Fuad Hussein, the chief of staff of the Kurdish forces, who told Patrick Cockburn of The Independent that ISIS had at least 200,000 fighters and the CIA's estimates were far too low.[72] Unfortunately for the Obama Administration and his CIA, this 200,000 figure may also be too low. This 200,000 fighter figure only takes into account where the fighting is occurring – in Libya, Syria and Iraq. In the five years since the disastrous Libyan invasion, the movement has metastasized and gone

---

[71] "ISIS driving up fighter numbers in Iraq, Syria: CIA," *english.alarabiya.net*, Sept. 12, 2014.
[72] P. Cockburn, "War with Isis: Islamic militants have army of 200,000, claims senior Kurdish leader," *independent.co.uk*, Nov. 14, 2014.

far past these three countries. ISIS operatives are presently active throughout Europe, Africa and parts of Asia and even the U. S. Any optimistic Obama administration official who thinks this movement will be controlled in the near future is a dreamer.

Thus, NATO forces attacked Libya, a sovereign, African nation, deposed and murdered its leader Muammar Gaddafi without any trial and that within five years this action resulted in a massive increase in ISIS' worldwide numbers. Many thousands of citizens of all races and religions have been murdered raped, tortured, imprisoned, kidnapped and even thrown off buildings by these terrorists. The fact that NATO does nothing without the approval of the US, places the blame for this international disaster and war crimes on the leader of the U. S., Barack Obama. However, he had a key ally in this effort.

A report by The New York Times on February 27, 2016 based on interviews of more than 50 officials from the US, Europe and Libya has shed new light on the background of this decision.[73] This report portrayed Hillary Clinton as the "major catalyst in the decision to go to war. In the run-up to the intervention, Clinton became convinced that overthrowing Gaddafi would lead to a democracy, according to multiple sources interviewed by The New York Times."[74]

"Former Secretary of Defense Robert Gates said Ms. Clinton was a major influence in President Obama's decision to go to war. Gates recounted Obama once telling him that the issue was split '51-49'. I've always thought that Hillary's support for the broader mission in Libya put the president on the 51 side of the line for a more aggressive approach," Gates said. "Can I finish the two wars I'm already in before you guys go looking for a third one?," Gates recalled saying.[75] Ms. Clinton also escalated the intervention in winning the debate over whether to arm the rebels. "Humvees, counterbattery radar, TOW missiles was the highest end we talked about. We were definitely giving them lethal assistance. We'd crossed that line," a State Department

---

[73] J. Becker & S. Shane, *supra.*
[74] *Id.;* "Role of Hillary Clinton in Libya war exposed," *rt.com*, March 3, 2016.
[75] *Id.*

official told The New York Times.[76]

RT America reported that "investigative journalist Gareth Porter called *The New York Times* report and Ms. Clinton's push for regime change in Libya 'part of a broader story in which she was really positioning herself to run for president. So we have both Libya and Syria on her secretaryship as indications of just how seriously we need to take her penchant for adventurism in foreign policy,'" Porter added.[77] Libya remains a failed basket case of a nation today with ISIS pockets in the north and the U. S. again dropping bombs on the region. The UN estimates 400,000 people have been displaced as a result of the intervention.[78]

As reported by Joel Gillin in *The New Republic*[79] on May 27th, 2015, Ms. Clinton said in an interview in 2011: "Imagine we were sitting here and Benghazi had been overrun. A city of 700,000 people, and hundreds of thousands had fled. . . . The cries would be, 'Why did the United States not do anything?'" Gillin continues:

> "It was the argument President Obama would also use to justify the no-fly zone put forward in U.N. Resolution 1973, which called for "all necessary measures" to protect civilians. Several reports have noted the pivotal role played by Clinton in convincing the president to support the intervention, which was also strongly backed by then-U.S. Ambassador to the U.N., Susan Rice, and Samantha Power, then serving at the National Security Council, as well as then Senator John Kerry, who invoked Rawanda."

However, Gillin notes that members of the intelligence community as reported in The Washington Times indicated that no solid intelligence existed to back up Ms. Clinton's claims. In essence, Hillary was making

---

[76] J. Becker & S. Shane, *supra.*
[77] "Role of Hillary Clinton in Libya war exposed," *supra.*
[78] *Source:* UN Refugee Agency.
[79] "Benghazi Won't Stick to Hillary Clinton, But the Disastrous Libyan Intervention Should," *newrepublic.com*, May 27, 2015.

up the likely potential abuse of Libyan citizens to bolster her presidential resume. Gillin quotes journalist Issandr El Amrani, a journalist "Was the threat to civilian life hyped up? It was probably exaggerated by Western officials."[80]

The Obama Administration clearly was not responsible for the creation of ISIS. Many different events and villains contributed to this, but the President's policies were definitely responsible for its rapid and enormous growth. Normally the president would be solely responsible for this, but in this case Ms. Clinton was the main driving force of this foreign policy. This would not be a major issue in most years, but this particular year, Ms. Clinton is running to be our next president and many of her supporters point to her experience in foreign policy as the main reason they are supporting her.

There is more than enough irony to go around in this kooky, chaotic cacophony masquerading as foreign policy. The most striking example of this is the fact that two of the largest contributors to the Clinton Foundation are Saudi Arabia and Qatar.[81] Saudi Arabia is the home base of Wahabbism, the ideology that inspired Al Qaeda and then ISIS.

If Bill and Hillary Clinton put together a list of their most cherished core beliefs and compared it to the corresponding Saudi-Qatari list, there would be few if any matches. The damning question then is why did these two countries give millions to The Clinton Foundation? Was it a thank you to Ms. Clinton for her foreign policy actions as Secretary of State that led to the advancement of the Saudi interests?

---

[80] J. Gillin, *supra*.
[81] J. Rubin, "Foreign donations to foundation raise major ethical questions for Hillary Clinton," *washingtonpost.com*, Feb. 18, 2015.

8.   Refugees on the Move

The European refugee crisis is a direct result of the chaos in Libya and Syria. The fall of Gaddafi made Libya a target destination for refugees seeking a short crossing into Italy. Well over a hundred thousand refuges have entered Europe from Libya.

The sudden entrance into Europe of well over a million refugees from far different cultures has created turmoil in the various European states that have taken them in. This was typified by the report of widespread sexual molestation that occurred in Cologne Germany on New Year's Eve. On that night, there were over a thousand victims and more than 2000 perpetrators from the Middle East.[82]

The largest number of refugees comes from Syria.[83] Germany has received more refugees than any other state, close to 500,000.[84] Tiny Hungary has received the second largest number, causing political and social disruption there. Though the United Kingdom has only accepted a small number of refugees, the threat of being forced to accept large numbers in the future may have been a factor in the recent vote to leave the European Union.

As discussed in Chapter 12, the pressure on the United States to accept large number of refugees has become a major issue in the

---

[82] R. Noack, "Leaked document says 2,000 men allegedly assaulted 1,200 German women on New Year's Eve," *Washington Post*, July 11, 2016.

[83] "Migrant crisis: Migration to Europe explained in seven charts," *bbc.com*, March 4, 2016.

[84] *Id.*

presidential election. Hillary Clinton takes the "open borders" position while Trump would essentially ban all Syrian refugees until such time as they can be vetted. Trump offers no details as to when that might be. Don't hold your breath.

This massive movement of peoples into countries with far different cultures, religious practices and political systems promises to cause upheaval in Europe and the United States for years to come.

9.   The U. S. Doubles Down

Undeterred by its previous policy failures in Libya, by the introduction of Russia into the equation, by the European refugee crisis and by the reality and threat of terrorist attacks on its homeland, the American government plunged recklessly ahead. Its intervention into Syria continued unabated.[85] However, it appeared that its emphasis had shifted to defeating the monster it helped create, ISIS.

It is in the nature of progressive politicians that they rarely if ever admit mistakes, particularly fundamental mistakes of policy as opposed to execution. The ultimate tool of all progressive policies, foreign or domestic, is the use of brute force to improve society. To admit that this methodology failed in some instances would threaten to call its efficacy per se into question. This they can never do as progressivism is not a rational system of thought but a means for providing a (false) sense of control over problems.[86] Questioning one progressive policy would threaten them all, instantly destroying the progressive's psychological house of cards.

This analysis fits Obama and Clinton perfectly. It is hard to think of any other politicians who have in their careers been less likely to admit to mistakes of any kind. They bring to mind Talleyrand's famous quip about the Bourbons: "They learn nothing." Rush Limbaugh has keenly observed about Obama that he acts as though he

---

85 Although the Pentagon is reported to have ended its program aiding alleged "moderate" rebels, the CIA continues to do so. See, M. Shear, H. Cooper & E. Schmitt, *"Obama Administration Ends Effort to Train Syrians to Combat ISIS,"* nytimes.com, OCT. 9, 2015.

[86] See, Progressivism: A Primer, *supra* at 21, *et seq.*

has not been the President for years when he speaks of matters over which he has had significant control and responsibility.

We have seen in America that progressives' refusal to end or abolish failed progressive policies have the nation in the midst of its first period of palpable decline since 1607 when the Jamestown colony was established. That same ignorant bullheadedness is even worse when it governs foreign relations as it leads to endless war and destruction.

10.   Russia Reacts

Russia had been aiding Syria from early on in the civil war with large supplies of military equipment. However, in September, 2015, Russian personnel and aircraft became directly involved in the conflict.[87] Russia claimed its main target was ISIS, however its critics accused it of primarily attacking anti-Assad rebels.

Long-time Middle East correspondent Robert Fisk, wrote, "The Russian air force in Syria has flown straight into the West's fantasy air space. The Russians, we are now informed, are bombing the 'moderates' in Syria – 'moderates' who even the Americans admitted two months ago, no longer existed."[88] The New York Times warned that Russian involvement against the rebels ranged against American support for the very same rebels created the risk of "an all-out proxy war" between the two superpowers.[89]

On October 31st, 2015 a Russian Metrojet was blown out of the sky over the Sinai. All 224 aboard were killed, including many children. ISIS claimed responsibility. This was the last straw for Putin. He began

---

[87] wikipedia.org/wiki/Russian_involvement_in_the_Syrian_Civil_War.
[88] "Syria's 'moderates' have disappeared... and there are no good guys," *independent.co.uk,* Oct. 4, 2015.
[89] A. Barnard & K. Shoumali, "U.S. Weaponry Is Turning Syria Into Proxy War With Russia," *nytimes.com,* Oct. 12, 2015.

a massive counter-offensive against ISIS in Syria, which has resulted in a loss of territory at least inside Syria for ISIS forces.

On February 22nd, 2016 an article written by Jay Syrmopoulos reported that a source close to Russian President Vladimir Putin has informed award-winning journalist Robert Parry that Putin has warned Turkey (a US ally) that any attempted ground invasion of Syria will be met with the defensive use of tactical nuclear weapons on the battlefield:

> "The Russian threat to use tactical nukes in the event of a joint Turkish-Saudi invasion should be taken extremely seriously given the duo's recent failed attempts to garner U. S. support for a ground invasion under the guise of aiding refugees and assisting 'moderate rebels'. In reality, this is simply a non-threatening label for the group's preferred Islamic extremist organizations in the Syrian theater of war. Moscow's warning comes on the heels of Saudi Foreign Minister Adel al-Jubeir telling CNN that Syrian President Assad must be removed 'by force' if a diplomatic solution fails."[90]

Syrmopoulos believes that "Russian intervention has decimated all insurgent groups on the ground and helped solidify the internationally recognized government's control over the war-torn country. . . "

In addition to increasing the risk of world war, including nuclear war, the Russian intervention has been an apparent success for Russia on a number of fronts. Columnist Frida Ghitis has identified several significant gains for Russia:

- "Russia is taunting Turkey, hoping for a crack in NATO unity."

- "Russia is courting the Syrian Kurds, threatening

---

[90] "Putin Threatens Turkey & Saudi Arabia with Tactical Nuclear Response to Syrian Ground Invasion," *thefreethoughtproject.com*.

American links to important allies in the fight against ISIS."

- "Russia's actions are contributing to a continuing and growing wave of Syrian refugees, with repercussions for the United States and its allies."

- "Russia, by helping create more refugees from Syria, is helping divide Europe against itself."[91]

Ghitis concludes by stating that "perhaps one day Putin will regret intervening in Syria. For now, as his forces bomb hospitals in Syria, and his supporters in Moscow call on the United Nations to punish Obama, Putin can only marvel at the success of his Syrian operation. Not only has he saved Assad from what was starting to look like the end of his rule, but he has also weakened the United States, its allies, and its alliances."

Recently, with the success of Brexit, Ghitis's analysis of the impact on Russian intervention in helping to divide Europe, has been confirmed.

In another ironic note, some involved in this evolving drama might well welcome a Russian-U.S. confrontation. With both out of the way, the goal of a worldwide Caliphate would no longer be a pipe dream.

---

[91] "Russia is using Syria to run circles around U.S.," *cnn.com*, Feb. 23, 2016.

11.   The Terrorists Respond

Terrorism is the weapon of the weak. ISIS responded to American and Russian military operations against it with just that weapon. On October 31, 2015, Russian Metrojet Flight 9268 crashed after an apparent bomb exploded on board, killing 217 passengers and seven crew members. ISIS claimed responsibility.[92]

ISIS claimed responsibility for a massive series of attacks in Paris on November 13, 2015 that shocked the Western world. The terrorists murdered 130 people and injured 368 more.[93] ISIS stated that the attacks were in retaliation for French airstrikes against ISIS in Iraq and Syria.[94] The French government responded with a war-time-like state of emergency which granted them extraordinary powers including banning public demonstrations.[95] It also continued if not intensified its air strikes against ISIS.

The violence came to the United States on December 2, 2015, when two probable ISIS sympathizers, perhaps acting on their own,

---

[92] See, wikipedia.org/wiki/Metrojet_Flight_9268.

[93] *Source*: Wikipedia.

[94] See, R. Callimachi, "ISIS Claims Responsibility, Calling Paris Attacks 'First of the Storm,'" *nytimes.com*, Nov. 14, 2015.

[95] D. Severson, State of Emergency: How the Paris Attacks Expanded France's Police Powers," *lawfareblog.com*, Nov. 15, 2015.

shot and killed 14 people and wounded 22 at a government office in San Bernardino, California, The shooters were a naturalized citizen from Pakistan and his wife, a lawful resident alien also from Pakistan.[96] ISIS struck again in Brussels on March 22, 2016, killing 32 and injuring 300.

War and terrorism are mutually reinforcing. War sparks terrorism which encourages an intensified military response which in turn stimulates an intensification of terrorist attacks. It is an arms race of violence between the forces of archism--states and would be-states--with civilians the biggest losers.

Neither the warring states nor their terrorist enemies seem to have the slightest clue how to create peace on earth. The cycle of violence unleashed in large part by the civil war in Syria is likely to continue so long as *might makes right* continues to be the predominant ideology of all sides to the conflict.

---

[96] wikipedia.org/wiki/2015_San_Bernardino_attack.

12.   Impact on the Presidential Election

The events in Europe and the Middle East quickly found their way into the American presidential election. The refugee crisis in Europe appeared to provide a boost to the anti-immigrant candidacy of Donald Trump. He had already gained support by promising to halt illegal immigration from Mexico. He reacted to the San Bernardino shooting by announcing a controversial temporary ban on Muslim immigrants traveling to the United States. The media thought Trump had committed political suicide by this pronouncement, however, his poll numbers shot up and polls revealed plenty of support for Trump's position among registered Republicans. Trump also made the defeat of ISIS a major plank in his platform but he declined to specify how this would be accomplished.

Trump became perhaps the first major political figure in America to call Hillary Clinton to account for her role in Libya and Syria. Though the real estate developer and political novice was widely thought to be unsophisticated in foreign policy, he was somehow able to notice what almost all mainstream analysts and politicians had missed, the massive Obama/Clinton policy failures in Libya and Syria. Trump said on Fox News Sunday:

> "She is the one that caused all this problem with her stupid policies," he said. "You look at what she did

with Libya, what she did with Syria. Look at Egypt, what happened with Egypt, a total mess. They don't back — we don't back any of our allies. You look, she was truly, if not 'the,' one of the worst secretary of states in the history of the country. She talks about me being dangerous. She's killed hundreds of thousands of people with her stupidity."

"What do you mean, hundreds of thousands?" [Chris] Wallace responded.

"She was secretary of state. Obama was president, the team," Trump said. "Two real geniuses."[97]

Hillary lamely responded, "Now is Libya perfect? It isn't. But did they have two elections that were free and fair where they voted for moderates. Yes, they did."[98] Bernie Sanders, true to form, criticized both Trump and Hillary in terms that made you wonder what the heck he was talking about:

> "We need a foreign policy based on building coalitions and making certain that the brave American men and women in our military do not get bogged down in perpetual warfare in the Middle East. That's what I will fight for as president."[99]

Most recently, Trump has been forced to explain his prior remarks appearing to support taking out Gaddafi with a surgical strike.[100] Hillary's illegal interventions into Libya and Syria promise to be major issues in the campaign, however, Trump's pragmatism, that is, his lack

---

[97] K. Robillard, "Trump: Hillary's killed 'hundreds of thousands,'" *Politico.com*, 12/13/15.

[98] D. Merica, "Clinton campaign defends Libya comment in face of RNC attacks," *CNN.com*, March 15, 2016.

[99] H. Neidig, "Sanders jabs at Clinton's foreign policy credentials following speech," *thehill.com*, June 2, 2016.

[100] "'Surgical shot to take out Gaddafi': Trump explains how he would have 'solved' Libya," *rt.com*, June 6, 2016.

of a coherent vision of foreign policy, inhibits his ability to capitalize on Hillary's horrible track record.

13.   The Risk of World War

Among the consequences of American intervention into Syria was a decision by Russia to intervene on behalf of its long-time ally, Syria. This development put the two nuclear powers at odds on a battlefield for the first time since Vietnam where Russia's predecessor the Soviet Union backed North Vietnam. However, the Syrian confrontation was and continues to be more dangerous as it creates the risk of direct conflict between the Russian military and American forces. Thus, the risk of nuclear war between the two leading nuclear powers was increased and for no good policy reason.

Neither state would deliberately start a nuclear war against the other. Rather, such a conflict would be the result of confusion, chaos and misunderstanding. As Eric Margolis explains, "It's also inevitable that land, sea and air provocations against Russia will eventually result in accidental clashes and a stern Russian response. All one needs is a Sarajevo II terror incident to spark a big shooting war between nuclear powers."[101]

The Syrian conflict contains the seeds of such problems. There are numerous different actors including the two superpowers, the Assad regime, Turkey and several different rebel groups. It was recently reported that the Pentagon was backing one rebel group while the CIA was backing another rebel group at war with the other.[102]

---

[101] "Stop Sabre-Rattling Before It's Too Late," *lewrockwell.com*, June 27, 2016.

[102] N. Bulos, W. Hennigan and B. Bennett, "In Syria, militias armed by the Pentagon fight those armed by the CIA," *LATimes.com*, Mar. 27, 2016.

"The attacks by one U. S.-backed group against another come amid continued heavy fighting in Syria and illustrate the difficulty facing U. S. efforts to coordinate among dozens of armed groups that are trying to overthrow the government of President Bashar Assad, fight the Islamic State militant group and battle one another all at the same time."[103]

Turkey, a U. S. ally, has already shot down a Russian plane. Had Russia chosen to retaliate against Turkey, the United States would have faced pressure to join the fight and further escalation would have been likely.

As of July, 2016, no one knows how any of this will end. What we do know is that Barack Obama and Hillary Clinton helped it to begin.

---

[103] *Id.*

14. Progressive Foreign Policy Fails Again

What happened in Libya and Syria is simply a manifestation of a very dangerous mindset known as progressivism. Progressivism amounts to a blind faith that government force can improve any given situation. It is usually associated with domestic policy but progressivism also operates in foreign policy. Progressives ignore costs and consequences. Progressives plunge into situations they do not understand, heedless of the consequences. When progressives fail, they invariably attribute the failure to not using enough government force. Thus, Obama, explaining his failure in Libya, stated, "I think we underestimated . . . the need to come in full *force*."[104]

Thus, it is not merely Obama and Clinton who need to be held responsible. Their underlying ideology also needs to be called to account. We need to *impeach progressivism too* lest that dangerous ideology leads us into an endless series of future foreign policy disasters as it has already led us into 100 years filled with them.

It is important to understand that a callous disregard of consequences is intrinsic to progressivism,[105] whether applied to domestic or foreign policy. One consequence of foreign intervention which the progressives utterly ignore is *blowback* in the form of terrorist attacks in direct retaliation against the intervention. It is probably a Freudian slip that those who supported overthrowing Gaddafi and

---

[104] T. Friedman, "Obama on the World," *nytimes.com*, Aug. 8, 2014 (emphasis added); *Progressivism: A Primer, supra* at 21, *et seq.*
[105] And archism as well.

Assad were oblivious to the consequences as these men had few ties to terrorism in recent years. However, if all that was said about them was true, then they should have been concerned about such retaliation. There is no similar excuse concerning ISIS, however. And true to form, *ISIS has delivered*, in Paris, in the skies of Egypt and in San Bernardino and Orlando. As of November of 2015, ISIS had engaged in over 1500 terrorist attacks.[106]

Another consequence of war that is rarely discussed in advance is the *legal* risk of engaging in war. When a state is attacked, it has the legal right to respond and defend itself.[107] Such a response may include attacking any military facility in the attacking state. Obviously, any such attacks in modern war run the risk of civilian casualties. Since this is rarely if ever mentioned by politicians, they apparently expect us to simply put all of this out of our minds.

What is truly revolting is this. Obama and Clinton, who are protected by heavy security, have launched the United States into wars against parties likely to retaliate against innocent and vulnerable civilians, when the perpetrators of these illegal wars are utterly incapable of stopping such attacks or protecting such civilians. *The only legal remedy for such moral depravity is impeachment.*

Although *foreign* progressivism is a species of the same genus as *domestic* progressivism, it is important to understand that foreign progressivism is even worse. Foreign progressive intervention has several features that differ from the domestic variety. First, progressives know even less about foreign lands than they do about their own country where they still make huge policy blunders. They are particularly unaware of the age-old conflicts among racial, ethnic and religious groups. They bring with them a western-style assumption, rooted in archism, that national borders are rational, just and sacrosanct. Thus, they are blind to the fact that the state boundaries in most parts of the world are unjust, arbitrary and usually imposed by imperial powers after violent conquest. Of course, as progressives

---

[106] M. Keneally & J. Diehm, "Sobering Chart Shows ISIS Is the Terror Group With Most Mass Killings Since 2000," *abcnews.go.com*, Nov 16, 2015.

[107] See, United Nations Charter, Article 51.

(and archists), the notion that states need to be broken up into smaller parts that would allow the various warring tribes and groups to run their own nations, is loathsome to them. Centralization is a primary progressive value. So, for example, after the U. S. conquest of the artificial state of Iraq, they insisted on its continued integrity. It was thus predictable that the Shiite majority would control the entire state after elections and impose its will on the minority Sunnis and Kurds, leading to the inevitable civil war. Hillary Clinton, who voted for the Iraq War, was herself blissfully unaware of this inevitability.

Second, people in foreign lands have never approved in any way the progressives' intervention into their own country. Third, that being the case, while domestic intervention has a number of tools at its disposal, foreign intervention has only one primary tool, war. War involves killing people and destroying property. Not only does this directly engender resistance and retaliation but it also strips away the protective coating of propaganda that usually cloaks state action. For example, since most people comply with tax laws, the state only rarely has to use actual force to collect them. Thus, the violent nature of taxation is hidden underneath the usual avalanche of birth-to-death progressive propaganda. For example, it is based on voluntary compliance; it is the citizens' duty, and it's all good because it was democratically approved. While all these rationalizations are nonsense, it is not easy to cut through the propaganda when the audience spent twelve years in a government school being brainwashed. In sharp contrast, when a bomb blows up an apartment building and kills thirty people, the facts are plain and the ability of propaganda to make people think that black is white, is minimal. Naturally, they tend to react, resist and retaliate.

To sum up, progressivism fails in foreign policy for a number of important reasons. First, the progressives are pervasively ignorant about the countries they are invading and conquering. Second, such intervention fails to deal with the underlying causes of problems, usually being related to the preexisting culture and character of a people or the arbitrary borders into which disparate ethnic, racial and religious groups have been consigned. Third, such intervention sparks resistance and retaliation among the victims. Finally, such intervention usually results in unforeseen and unintended bad consequences.

Thus, the lesson of this book is not just that Obama and Clinton blundered by intervening into Libya and Syria but that, once again, progressives applied their utopian theory beyond the borders of the United States with the usual disastrous consequences.

15. The Case for Impeachment

The Framers intended impeachment to be used frequently to check the extensive powers of the executive and thus the executive's tendency to abuse that power. The President's explicit powers are enormous. Through custom and practice and under the influence of the ideology of progressivism that places a high value on centralized power, those powers have expanded even further. Yet, impeachment has had little impact on recent history. With the exception of the commencement of impeachment proceedings against Richard Nixon and the actual impeachment and acquittal of Bill Clinton, impeachment has been largely absent from American politics in recent decades.

It can even be argued that the lack of use of impeachment has led us to our current plight. For generations, and significantly in the progressive era, 1912 through the present, presidents have basically done whatever they want with respect to war and covert foreign action without fear of impeachment. Wilson, FDR, Truman, LBJ, Nixon, Bush I, Clinton, Bush II and Obama have engaged in various illegal, dishonest, immoral, and just plain stupid foreign wars and covert actions while paying no legal price. Ironically, Clinton was impeached not for engaging in a war against Serbia without a declaration of war but for lying about sex. This Congressional lenience and inaction has encouraged Presidents, including obviously Obama and potential president Clinton to think they can do whatever the hell they want in foreign affairs.

The threat of impeachment has been largely reserved for blowing off steam against presidents whose policies we dislike. Like the *Boy Who Cried Wolf*, the many threats of impeachment have served to discredit the general concept. The impeachment of Clinton also degraded the concept as many perceived that he was being impeached largely because of a personal hatred of him and not for any offense that would merit impeachment. Lying about having sex with a young intern, when such lies appeared to be part of a partisan perjury trap and which did not involve actual official misconduct, is not grounds for impeachment. Alas, as the tale of the *Boy Who Cried Wolf* illustrates, sometimes there actually is a wolf. Sometimes, there actually are high crimes that merit impeachment. This book has made that case.

We can quickly rule out legal options other than impeachment. In theory, officials who wage war without legal authority could be prosecuted for crimes either domestically or under international law. Neither is going to happen. The U. S. Justice Department, run by an Obama appointee, is not going to indict President Obama or Hillary Clinton for murder or lesser crimes. Realistically, such prosecutions are only aimed at low-ranking officials. The same is true under international law. "International law simply doesn't apply to the big powers or their political leaders," writes Seumas Milne.[108] All 28 people charged by the International Criminal Court have been from Africa.[109] Obama and Clinton are, as they say, "too big to jail." Impeachment, a procedure controlled by a separate branch of government, the Congress, is the only feasible option for justice.

Should impeachment be avoided for a president who is near the end of his term? Obviously not! Should such a rule or custom be adopted, it would be tantamount to giving that officeholder a free ride to engage in misconduct so long as it is timed to occur late in his term. Even if an official is removed near the end of his term, such a penalty provides justice in that instance and creates a powerful deterrent effect against misconduct by future officeholders.

---

[108] S. Milne, *supra.*
[109] *Id.*

Is it proper to impeach someone who has recently been elected? Yes! Every impeachment involves the removal of an elected official and is therefore undemocratic in a technical sense. However, the very Constitution that allows this to happen, and which allows for the election in the first place, was also voted on democratically and can be changed at any time through democratic procedures.

Yes, but impeaching Hillary Clinton flies in the face of the right of the people to vote for the candidate of their choosing and by voting for her, they have already "vetted" her on Libya and Syria. False! First of all, the argument assumes that the voters had access to all relevant information and the truth was not smothered to death by a complex web of lies. All of the available evidence is to the contrary. See, Chapters 3 and 5. More importantly, the majority of the people who bother to show up on election day do not have the right to install a candidate who is guilty of war crimes.

No reasonable person can deny that *some* evil deeds, even if committed before an election, are sufficient to override the choice of the voters. So, the question is not, as it might first appear, whether such an impeachment is *proper in principle*, but whether it is *proper under these circumstances*. The evidence for that proposition, as already set forth in this book, is overwhelming. There is no legal, moral or logical reason to take the impeachment of a recently elected candidate off the table as a matter of principle.

Finally, should the unlikelihood of impeachment deter serious proposals for impeachment? Obviously not. The current Congress, which itself bears major responsibility for illegal and unwise American interventions into the Middle East, is without a doubt highly unlikely to initiate impeachment proceedings based on the charges outlined in this book. However, the possibility cannot be ruled out as stranger things have happened. Further, if the case is presented to Congress and rejected, it then becomes possible *to hold Congress accountable* for their calculated disregard of their duties through public disapprobation, electoral opposition and ostracism[110] in their districts.

The positing of serious impeachment charges can also serve to educate the public about the crimes their elected officials have

---

[110] See, James Ostrowski, *Direct Citizen Action*, p. 44.

perpetrated. While the public cannot itself impeach elected officials, it can consider such charges in casting its votes for both the presidency *and* Congress. Of course, in this instance, there is the happy coincidence that one of the perpetrators of these high crimes is herself currently a candidate for president!

Obama is of course not on the ballot this year but a young, ambitious man like Obama surely has plans to stay in the game of politics, perhaps seeking to head the United Nations. If this indictment of his high crimes on the world stage can deprive him of that prize and taint his post-presidential career, that will be a small measure of justice. It is true that there is no absolute justice in this imperfect world but we should not let the perfect be the enemy of the good. We should not allow miscreants like Obama to be let off the hook. As Victor Hugo wrote, "increasing the magnitude of a crime cannot be its diminution."[111]

We ask the House of Representatives to investigate whether there is clear and convincing evidence to believe that:

I.   The Respondents knowingly and intentionally and unlawfully waged war against Libya without a declaration of war from Congress and in the absence of any immediate threat to the security of the United States.

II.   The Respondents knowingly and intentionally used false information to persuade the United Nations Security Council to pass Resolution 1973 that approved the creation of a no-fly zone over Libya.

III.   The Respondents knowingly and intentionally waged war against the Libyan regime in a manner that far exceeded the scope of UN Resolution 1973.

---

[111] Oration on Voltaire.

IV.   The Respondents knowingly and intentionally waged war against Syria without a declaration of war from Congress and without any immediate threat to the security of the United States.

V.   The Respondents knowingly and intentionally used false information to justify waging war against Syria.

The Legal Grounds for Impeachment

General principles. The Constitution states: "The President, Vice President and all civil officers of the United States, shall be removed from office on impeachment for, and conviction of, treason, bribery, or other high crimes and misdemeanors."[112] Impeachment is a "political question," meaning that decisions on impeachment will rarely if ever be overturned by the courts.[113] After considering various options, the Framers settled on an impeachment standard that was quite broad.[114]   Proof of a criminal act is not required for impeachment. The term "misdemeanor" as used in the text did not necessarily mean an actual crime at the time of the ratification. Rather, it meant "misdeed."[115] On the other hand, mere political disagreements should be insufficient.[116]   One of the best statements of the proper grounds for impeachment was made by North Carolina ratifier James Iredell: impeachment is appropriate in response to harm "arising from acts of great injury to the community."[117]

Engaging in war unauthorized by the Constitution. The President and Executive branch may not wage war unless that war is declared by

---

[112] Article II, section 4.

[113] *Nixon v. United States,* 506 U.S. 224 (1993).

[114] See, S. Presser, "Standards for Impeachment," The Heritage Guide to the Constitution, *Heritage.org.*

[115] *Id.*

[116] *Id.*

[117] Quoted by Presser, *Id.*

Congress or is necessary for the emergency defense of the United States.[118] An eminent constitutional scholar stated in 2007:

> "The president does not have power under the Constitution to unilaterally authorize a military attack in a situation that does not involve stopping an actual or imminent threat to the nation."[119]

That scholar later became President Barack Obama. Yet another prominent constitutional authority stated in 2007:

> "The president has no Constitutional authority to take this country to war against a country of seventy million people unless we're attacked or there is proof that we are about to be attacked and if he does, I would move to impeach him. The House obviously has to do that but I would lead an effort to impeach him. . . . I don't say it lightly. I don't say it lightly."

That scholar was Vice-President Joe Biden, long-time chairman of the Senate Judiciary Committee. As candidate Obama ran on an explicit platform of a narrow construction of presidential war powers, and, presumably received a large number of votes on that basis from a war-weary public, an additional ground for impeachment in his case is *defrauding the voters*. An official should not be heard to complain about

---

[118] See, e.g., "Rep. Tom McClintock explains why Obama's war in Libya is unconstitutional." *Cato.org* speech, April 7, 2011 (citing Federalist No. 69).

[119] See also, D. Kucinich, "The US must end its illegal war in Libya now," *theguardian.com*, July 9, 2011: "First, the war is illegal under the United States constitution and our War Powers Act, because only the US Congress has the authority to declare war and the president has been unable to show that the US faced an imminent threat from Libya. The president even ignored his top legal advisers at the Pentagon and the department of justice who insisted he needed congressional approval before bombing Libya."

impeachment overturning the results of an election when he is impeached for the very reason that his misconduct violated the promises he made in that election.

Yet another prominent American lawyer, Senator Tim Kaine,[120] summed up our present predicament if these practices continue with impunity:

> "And so at the end of this administration with the complicity of this Congress, I think we've basically come up with a war doctrine that says wherever and whenever as long as the president feels that it's a good idea without Congress even needing to do anything about it. I think that's become the rule — that's a rule I think will haunt us — domestically under future presidents and Congresses."[121]

UN Resolution 1973. This United Nations resolution did not constitutionally justify the Libyan intervention. The Washington Times, a pro-intervention paper, succinctly explained why in an editorial:

> "The U.N. resolution authorizes member states to take a number of military and nonmilitary actions to protect the people of Libya from Col. Gadhafi's government. Under its own rules, however, the United Nations cannot legally authorize military action to shape the internal affairs of member states. Article 2 section 7 of the U.N. charter states that, "Nothing contained in the present Charter shall authorize the United Nations to intervene in matters which are

---

[120] J. D., Harvard Law School (1983); clerked for Judge R. Lanier Anderson III of the United States Court of Appeals for the Eleventh Circuit (*source*: Wikipedia).

[121] K. Wong, "Dem senator compares Obama's moves in Syria to Putin's in Ukraine," *thehill.com*, April 28, 2016.

essentially within the domestic jurisdiction of any state or shall require the Members to submit such matters to settlement under the present Charter." Chapter VII of the charter, which enumerates U.N. intervention powers, applies only to international breaches of the peace. The December 1981 U.N. "Declaration on the Inadmissibility of Intervention and Interference in the Internal Affairs of States" reaffirmed this principle with its solemn declaration that, "No State or group of States has the right to intervene or interfere in any form or for any reason whatsoever in the internal and external affairs of other States."[122]

Another analyst points out that U. S. law, the United Nations Participation Act, requires Congressional approval of agreements with the U. N. security Council except in limited situations not relevant here.[123]

War Powers Act. The War Powers Act does not justify these interventions. As Conor Friedensdorf wrote in *The Atlantic* in 2011, "the situation in Libya was never a national emergency created by an attack on the United States. So President Obama was in violation of this law that he claims to uphold from the beginning."[124]

Using deception to gain support for war. As discussed in Chapter 3, the use of deception has been such a frequent strategy for dragging the nation into wars that this aspect of the perpetrators' misconduct should constitute separate and independent grounds for impeachment. At the same time, deception implies the existence of a hidden and usually insidious agenda that officials do not wish to disclose as its disclosure would lead the public to oppose the war. It is time to put a

---

[122] "Obama's Illegal War," March 18, 2011; see also, T. McLintock, *supra.*

[123] J. Vines, "Can the UN Allow Obama to Wage War?," *hypersyl.com,* April 10, 2011.

[124] "Obama Fails to Justify the Legality of War in Libya," *theatlantic.com,* June 16, 2011; see also, T. McKlintock, *supra.*

stop to these twin practices—deception and hidden agendas—by making them additional and significant grounds for impeachment.

Unlawful Expenditure of Appropriated Funds. Since the Libyan and Syrian interventions were not authorized and yet involved significant expenditures, such actions subverted the Constitution and usurped the powers of the Congress.[125] Again, there is an element here of overturning the voters' electoral choices and thus the perpetrators cannot be heard to complain that calling them to account for their malefactions is undemocratic. Rather, impeachment reinstates the democratic choices the voters made when electing the Congress that *chose not to* allocate funds for these misadventures.

Conor Friedersdorf quotes Rep. Bill Young (R-Fla.) in this regard:

> "Article I, section 9 of the Constitution, in part, reads, 'No money shall be drawn from the Treasury, but in consequence of appropriations made by law; and a regular statement and account of the receipts and expenditures of all public money shall be published from time to time.'... What I'm wondering is: Where is the money to pay for the Libyan operation coming from? What account is it coming from? Is it coming out of personnel costs--soldiers' pay? Is it coming out of medical care? Is it coming out of the training for our troops? What accounts are being used?"

As Congressman Young suggests, the transgression is two-fold, (1) spending money in an unauthorized manner and (2) stealing the funds from an authorized use approved by Congress.

Violations of International Law. Aggressive war is unlawful under international law. One of the reasons why Hitler is so reviled is that he engaged in aggressive war against other nations not in self-defense. War crimes are also unlawful under international law. Count two of the Nuremburg Indictment reads as follows:

---

[125] See also, C. Freidersdorf, *supra.*

"All the defendants with divers other persons, during a period of years preceding 8 May 1945, participated in the planning, preparation, initiation, and waging of wars of aggression, which were also wars in violation of international treaties, agreements, and assurances."

The Judgment at Nuremburg stated:

"To initiate a war of aggression, therefore, is not only an international crime; *it is the supreme international crime differing only from other war crimes in that it contains within itself the accumulated evil of the whole.*"[126]

Interestingly, Hillary Clinton actually gave a Nuremburg-style defense of her actions in Libya: "At the end of the day, this was the president's decision."[127] She was apparently just following orders.

The mass killing of civilians can be considered a war crime. Here, the perpetrators armed terrorist groups that were known to be engaging in atrocities against civilians.

Violation of U. S. Law. Murder is unlawful in the United States and in every other jurisdiction on the planet. Murder is the intentional killing of a human being without legal justification. Justification can include self-defense or authorization under constitutional war powers. In the absence of justification, such killing is *murder.* It has already been established that the interventions into Libya and Syria were unlawful. Thus, any acts of intentional killing or aiding and abetting intentional killing in those interventions were arguably murder and thus grounds for impeachment.

The very same analysis applies to the well-established crime of providing material support to terrorist organizations. See 18 U.S. Code § 2339B. Unless this behavior is somehow legally justified, it is unlawful. Since this conduct was not justified by the Constitution or by a need to defend the United States against imminent attack, it is unlawful and therefore grounds for impeachment.

---

[126] avalon.law.yale.edu/imt/judnazi.asp (emphasis added).
[127] J. Becker & S. Shane, *supra.*

Numerous other crimes were committed as a direct result of the intervention into Libya and Syria such as assault, kidnapping, rape and massive destruction of property. Again, in the absence of any legal justification, these become serious prosecutable crimes and thus grounds for impeachment.

Summary. The basic facts of the indictment against Obama and Clinton have been set forth in Chapters 3 and 5. The devastating consequences have been detailed in Chapters 4, 6, 7, 8, 9, 10 and 13. The legal grounds for impeachment have been spelled out in this chapter. The case for impeachment has been made.

Conclusion

Two public officials, indulging the pernicious progressive fantasy that government force can cure all human ills, likely engaged in behavior that was unlawful and criminal and whose consequences have unleashed devastation across four continents. Yet, one of the perpetrators is, at the time of this publication, the favorite[128] to be the next president. The other, the incumbent president, is still a respected public figure even if his poll numbers have dipped.

No price has yet been paid. These malefactors have so far escaped justice. More importantly, *no lesson has been learned.* There has been no acknowledgement that these policies have failed. On the contrary, since government creates its own demand, the problems caused by the Libyan and Syrian interventions will likely be used as a justification for ever further interventions and wars in the Middle East and perhaps in Europe as well. The terrorist attacks that followed these interventions will be used as a rationalization for moving ever closer to a police state in America.

If public officials can openly and with impunity engage in unlawful and foolhardy foreign misadventures causing such disastrous consequences, then we can expect such behavior to continue in the very near future with unknown consequences including the possibility

---

[128] Based on the Real Clear Politics poll averages.

Conclusion

of endless terrorist attacks in the United States, the disintegration of Europe and even nuclear war with Russia.

It has been said that the only thing we learn from history is that we learn nothing from history. Perhaps the solution to that conundrum is that we need to stop merely learning from history and start making history.

Recommended Websites

Antiwar.com

ArtVoice.com (Buffalo, N. Y.)
(publisher of Jim Ostrowski's column)

Future of Freedom Foundation
(fff.org)

LewRockwell.com
(publisher of Jim Ostrowski's column)

LibertyMovement.org

Mises.org

RonPaulInstitute.org

ScottHorton.org

TargetLiberty.com

TomWoods.com

Index

About the Authors

Michael Ostrowski graduated from St. Joseph's Collegiate Institute (1970) where he was captain of the cross-country team. He received a degree in psychology from the State University of New York at Buffalo in 1975. He is a free-lance writer and partner at Morgit Talent in Long Island, New York.

James Ostrowski is a trial and appellate lawyer and libertarian writer from Buffalo, New York. He graduated from St. Joseph's Collegiate Institute in 1975 and obtained a degree in philosophy from the State University of New York at Buffalo in 1980 and a law degree from Brooklyn Law School in 1983. He has written a number of scholarly articles on the law and has written several bar association reports and given continuing legal education lectures on *habeas corpus*, lawsuits against government officials and jury nullification.